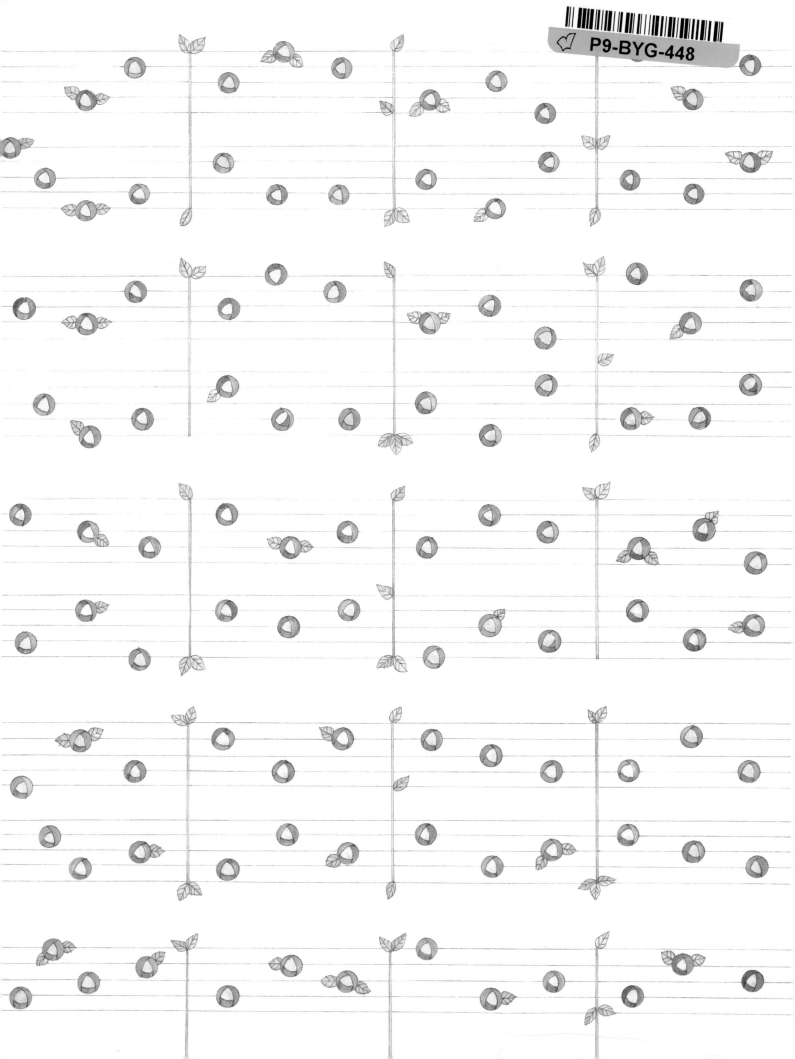

Grandmother Remembers

Songbook

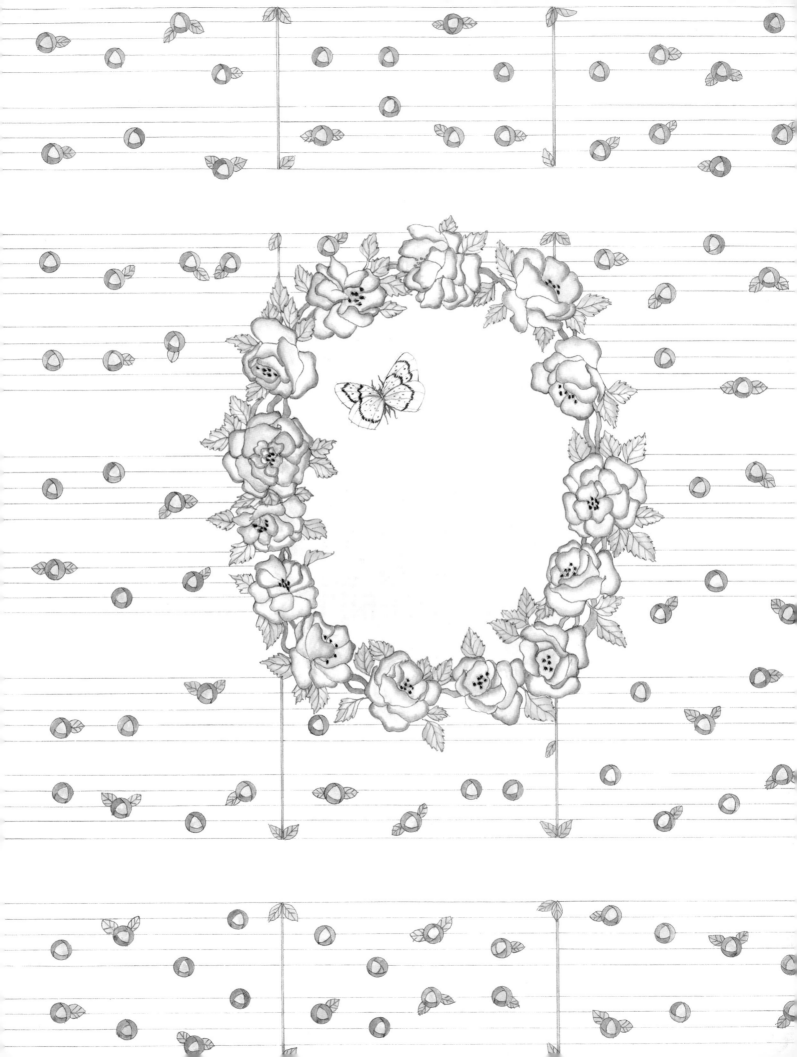

Grandmother Remembers

Songbook

Conceived and written by Judith Levy
Designed and illustrated by Judy Pelikan

A Welcome Book

Workman Publishing, New York

Library of Congress Cataloging-in-Publication Data
Grandmother remembers songbook / [compiled] by Judith Levy and Judy Pelikan.
    p. of music.
    For voice and piano (vocal part incorporated into piano part) with
chord symbols.
    Companion volume to: Grandmother remembers / Judith Levy.
    Summary: Words and music for thirty-nine songs including "Old MacDonald;"
"Skip to My Lou;" "Eency, Weency Spider;" and "London Bridge."
    ISBN 1-56305-316-0 (cloth) : $15.95
    1. Children's songs.   [1. Songs.]   I. Levy, Judith.
II. Pelikan, Judy.   III. Levy, Judith.   Grandmother remembers.
M1997.G798   1992   92-50287
                                                                         CIP
                                                              M   AC

Books are available at special discounts when purchased in bulk for premiums and sales promotions as well as
for fundraising or educational use. Special editions or book excerpts can also be created to specification.
For details, contact the Special Sales Director at the address below.

Workman Publishing, 708 Broadway, New York, NY 10003

Printed and bound in Singapore, first printing September 1992
10 9 8 7 6 5 4 3 2 1

Poems and songs I used to love,
When I was little, too.
It's so much fun to share them
With a grandchild sweet as you.

With love for _____

From _____

Date _____

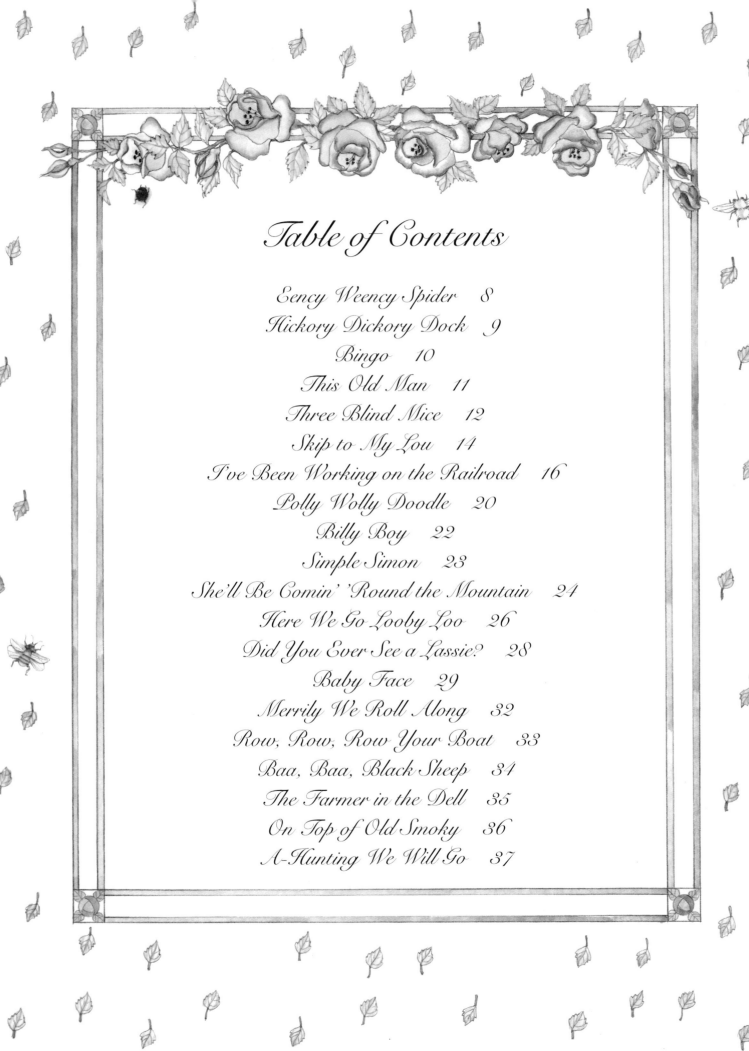

Table of Contents

Hickory Dickory Dock

Moderately

mf Hick - o - ry, dick - o - ry, dock, the

mouse ran up the clock. The

clock struck one and down he run;

Hick - o - ry, dick - o - ry, dock!

Bingo

Brightly

f There was a farm-er who had a dog, and Bing-o was his name - o.

B - I - N - G - O, B - I - N - G - O,

B - I - N - G - O, and Bing-o was his name - o.

For 2nd verse clap on the letter B. On the 3rd verse clap for B and I. Continue substituting claps for each letter in turn until five claps take the place of the B-I-N-G-O.

This Old Man

Bouncy

This old man, he played {one. two. three.} He played knick knack

on my {thumb. shoe. With a knee.} knick knack pad-dy whack, give a dog a bone,

For additional verses / *Last time*

this old man came roll-ing home. roll - ing home.

Continue similarly with
four . . . door . . .
five . . . hive . . .
six . . . sticks . . .
seven . . . up in heaven . . .
eight . . . gate . . .
nine . . . spine . . .
ten . . . over again . . .

Three Blind Mice

Skip to My Lou

Square dance tempo

mf

1. Fly in the but-ter-milk, shoo, fly, shoo!
2. Lost my __ part-ner, what'll I do?

Fly in the but-ter-milk, shoo, fly, shoo!
Lost my __ part-ner, what'll I do?

sim.

Fly in the but-ter-milk,
Lost my __ part-ner,

shoo, fly, shoo!
what'll I do?

Skip to my Lou, my dar - lin'.
Skip to my Lou, my dar - lin'.

3. Little red wagon, painted blue,
   Little red wagon, painted blue,
   Little red wagon, painted blue,
   Skip to my Lou, my darlin'.
        (Chorus)

4. Look at the greenie* standing there,
   Look at the greenie standing there,
   Look at the greenie standing there,
   Skip to my Lou, my darlin'.
        (Chorus)

5. Lost my partner, what'll I do?
   Lost my partner, what'll I do?
   Lost my partner, what'll I do?
   Skip to my Lou, my darlin'.
        (Chorus)

6. I'll get another one sweeter than you,
   I'll get another one sweeter than you,
   I'll get another one sweeter than you,
   Skip to my Lou, my darlin'.
        (Chorus)

*A greenie was an odd boy or girl, one without a partner.

I've Been Working on the Railroad

*Strum each chord lightly, like a guitar.

Billy Boy

3. Can she bake a cherry pie?
   She can bake a cherry pie
   Quick as she can wink her eye . . .

Simple Simon

She'll Be Comin' 'Round the Mountain

Brightly, with spirit

3. Oh, we'll all come down to greet her when she comes (when she comes).
   Oh, we'll all come down to greet her when she comes (when she comes).
   Oh, we'll all come down to greet her,
   Yes, we'll all come down to greet her,
   Oh, we'll all come down to greet her when she comes (when she comes).

4. Oh, we'll all sing "Hallelujah" when she comes (when she comes).
   Oh, we'll all sing "Hallelujah" when she comes (when she comes).
   Oh, we'll all sing "Hallelujah,"
   Yes, we'll all sing "Hallelujah,"
   Oh, we'll all sing "Hallelujah" when she comes (when she comes).

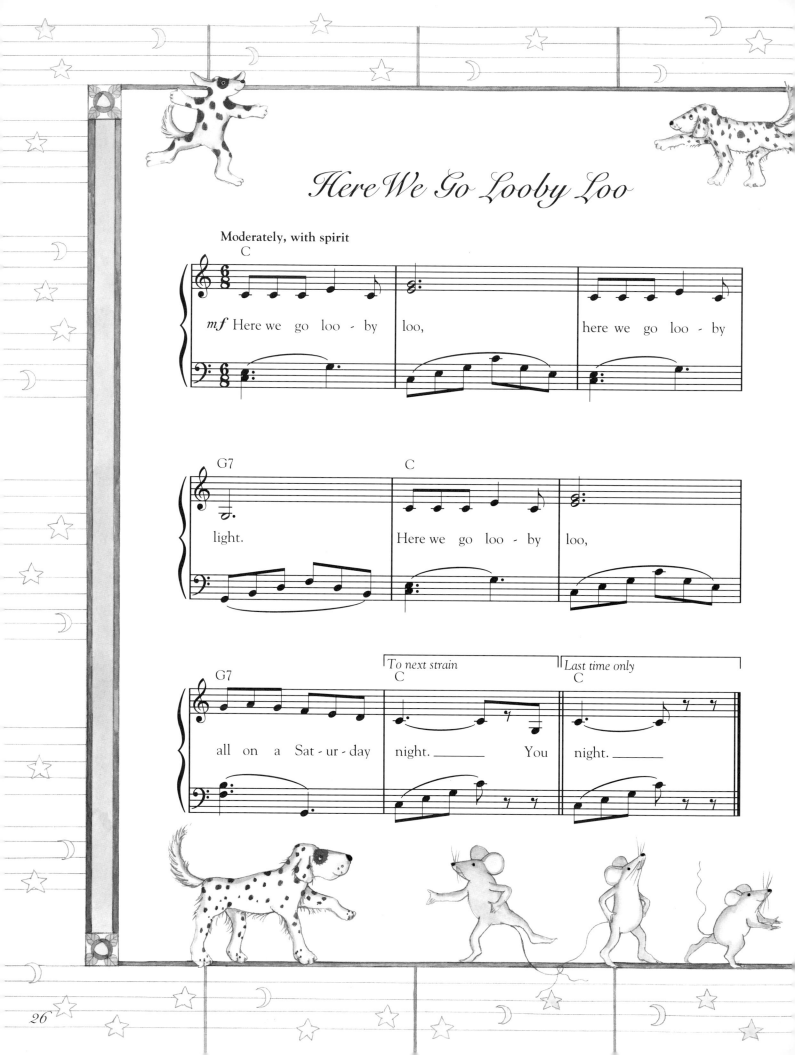

March

put your {left foot / right foot} in, you put your {left foot / right foot} out, you give your {left foot / right foot} a shake, then turn your-self a-bout.

sfz

D.C.

Continue similarly with
left hand . . .
right hand . . .
backside . . .
frontside . . .
whole self . . .

Did You Ever See a Lassie?

Moderately

mf Did you ev - er see a lass - ie, a lass - ie, a lass - ie? Did you
Did you ev - er see a lad - die, a lad - die, a lad - die? Did you

ev - er see a lass - ie go this way and that?⎱
ev - er see a lad - die go this way and that?⎰ Go

this way and that way and this way and that way? Did you

ev - er see a ⎱lass - ie⎰ go this way and that?
⎰lad - die⎱

Baby Face

Moderately

Ba - by face, you've got the cut - est lit - tle ba - by face. There's not an - oth - er one could take your place,

ba - by face, ___ my poor heart ___ is jump-in';

You sure have start - ed some-thin'. Ba - by face, ___

___ I'm up in heav - en when I'm

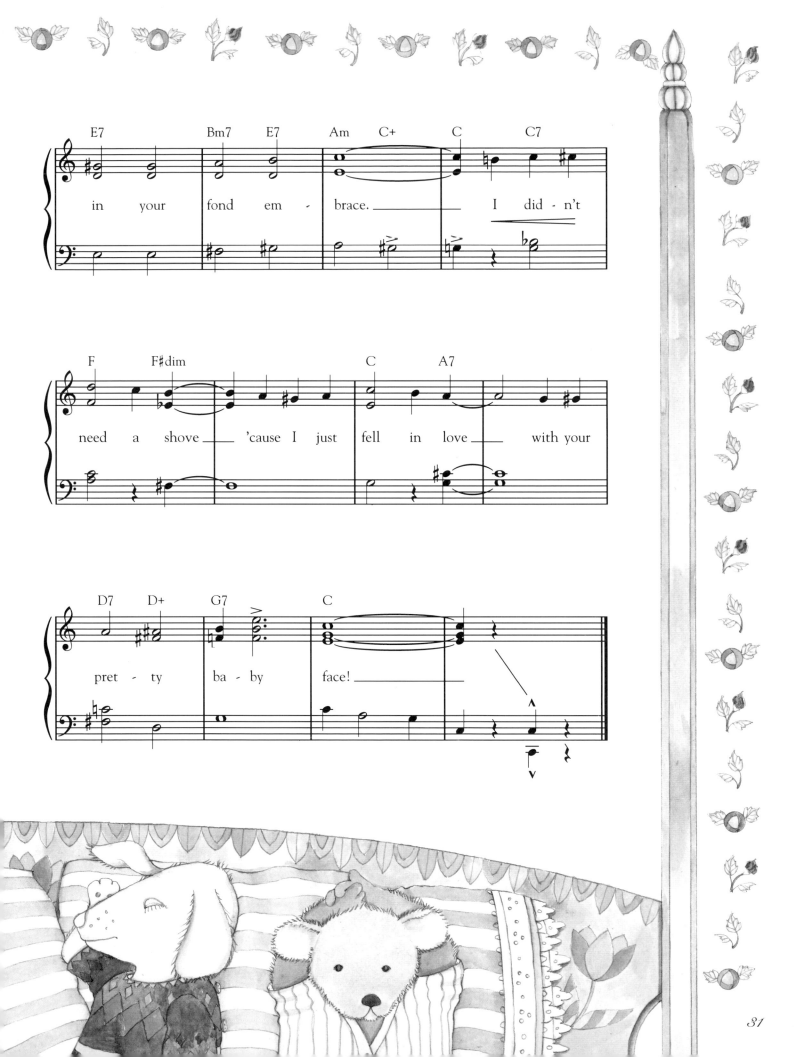

Merrily We Roll Along

Row, Row, Row Your Boat

*This song can be sung as a round.

The Farmer in the Dell

Allegretto

mf

1. The farm - er in the dell, _____ the
2. The farm - er takes a wife, _____ the

farm - er in the dell, _____ Hi, ho, the
farm - er takes a wife, _____ Hi, ho, the

dair - y - o, the farm - er in the dell. _____
dair - y - o, the farm - er takes a wife. _____

Continue similarly with
3. The wife takes the child . . .
4. The child takes a nurse . . .
5. The nurse takes the dog . . .
6. The dog takes the cat . . .
7. The cat takes the rat . . .
8. The rat takes the cheese . . .
9. The cheese stands alone . . .

On Top of Old Smoky

3. A thief he will rob you
   And take what you have,
   But a false-hearted lover
   Will lead you to your grave.

4. They'll hug you and kiss you
   And tell you more lies
   Than cross-ties on a railroad
   Or stars in the sky.

A-Hunting We Will Go

With spirit

mf A - hunt - ing we will go, a -

hunt - ing we will go, we'll catch a lit - tle fox and

put him in a box and then we'll let him go. _____

Buffalo Gals

Moderately

C

mf 1. As   I   was   walk - ing   down   the   street,
(2. I)   asked   her   would   she   have   some   talk,

G7   C

down   the   street,   down   the   street,   a   pret - ty   lit - tle   girl   I
have   some   talk,   have   some   talk.   I   asked   her   would   she

G7   C

chanced   to   meet.   Oh,   she   was   fair   to   see!
have   some   talk   as   she   stood   close   to   me.

Chorus

Buf-fa-lo gals won't you come out to-night, come out to-night, *sim.*

come out to-night? Buf-fa-lo gals won't you come out to-night and

dance by the light of the moon? 2. I moon?

3. I asked her would she like to dance,
   Like to dance, like to dance.
   I asked her would she like to dance
   As she stood close to me.
    (chorus)

4. I asked her if she'd be my wife,
   Be my wife, be my wife.
   Then I'd be happy all my life,
   If she'd marry me.
    (chorus)

Home on the Range

Yankee Doodle

With spirit

mf Yan-kee Doo-dle went to town, a - rid-ing on a po - ny. He

stuck a feath-er in his cap and called it mac-a - ro - ni!

f Yan - kee Doo-dle keep it up! Yan - kee Doo-dle dan - dy!

Mind the mu - sic and the step and with the girls be hand - y.

The Muffin Man

Bright and happy

Do you know the muf - fin man, the
Yes, I know the muf - fin man, the

muf - fin man, the muf - fin man?
muf - fin man, the muf - fin man.

Do you know the
Yes, I know the

muf - fin man who lives in Dru - ry Lane?
muf - fin man who lives in Dru - ry Lane.

Twinkle, Twinkle, Little Star

Where Is Thumbkin?

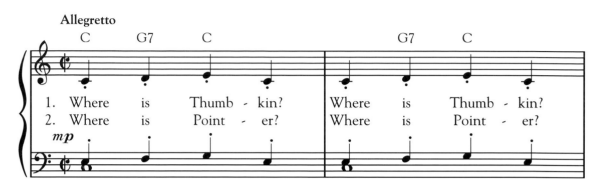

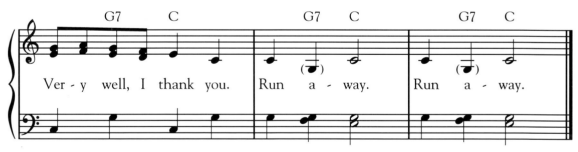

3. Where is Middle? Where is Middle?
   Here I am. Here I am.
   How are you today, sir?
   Very well, I thank you.
   Run away. Run away.

4. Where is Ringer? Where is Ringer?
   Here I am. . . .

5. Where is Pinkie? Where is Pinkie?
   Here I am. . . .

Where, Oh Where, Has My Little Dog Gone?

Plaintively

mp Where, oh where, has my lit - tle dog gone? Oh

where, oh where can he be? _____ With his

ears cut short and his tail cut long, Oh

where, oh where can he be? _____

Lazy Mary

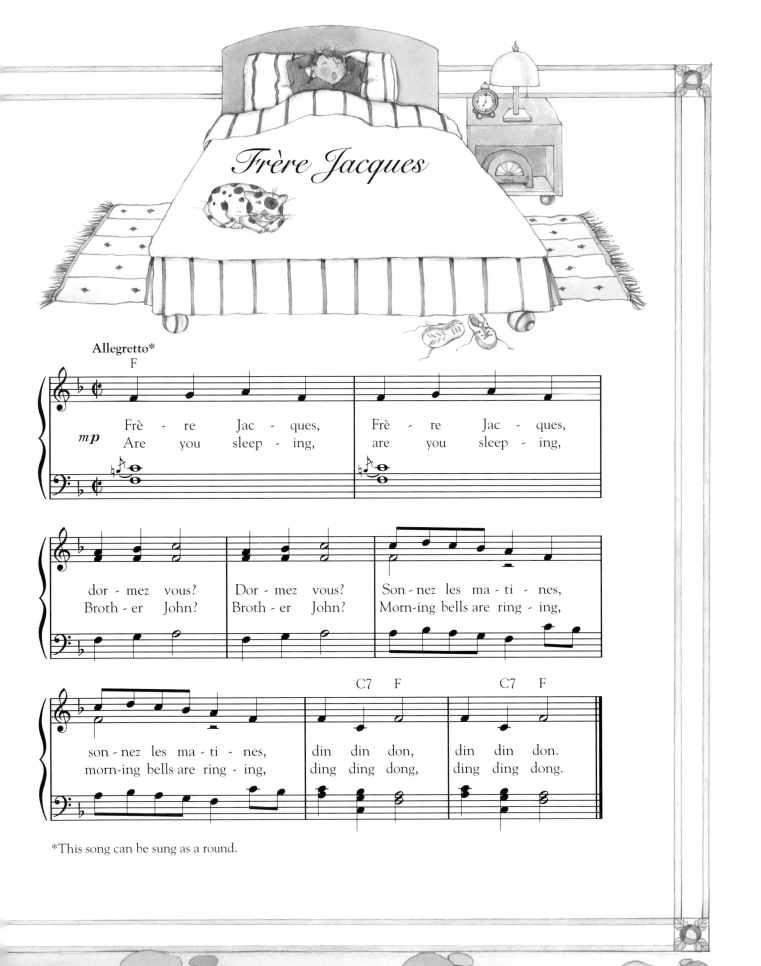

Allegretto*

*This song can be sung as a round.

Hot Cross Buns

London Bridge

Allegretto

1. Lon - don Bridge is fall - ing down, fall - ing down, fall - ing down. Lon - don Bridge is fall - ing down, my fair la - dy.

2. Build it up with i - ron bars, i - ron bars, i - ron bars. Build it up with i - ron bars, my fair la - dy.

3. Build it up with gold and silver,
Gold and silver, gold and silver.
Build it up with gold and silver,
My fair lady.

4. Take the key and lock her up,
Lock her up, lock her up.
Take the key and lock her up,
My fair lady.

Down by the Station

Rock-a-bye Baby

Gently

p Rock - a - bye ba - by on the tree - top,

when the wind blows the cra - dle will rock.

When the bough breaks the cra - dle will fall, and

down will come ba - by, cra - dle and all.

The Mulberry Bush

Moderately

mf

1. Here we go 'round the mul-ber-ry bush, the mul-ber-ry bush, the mul-ber-ry bush.
2. This is the way we wash our clothes, we wash our clothes, we wash our clothes.

Here we go 'round the mul-ber-ry bush so ear-ly in the morn-ing.
This is the way we wash our clothes so ear-ly Mon-day morn-ing.

3. This is the way we iron our clothes,
   We iron our clothes, we iron our clothes.
   This is the way we iron our clothes
   So early Tuesday morning.

4. This is the way we scrub the floor,
   We scrub the floor, we scrub the floor.
   This is the way we scrub the floor
   So early Wednesday morning.

5. This is the way we mend our clothes,
   We mend our clothes, we mend our clothes.
   This is the way we mend our clothes
   So early Thursday morning.

6. This is the way we sweep the house,
   We sweep the house, we sweep the house.
   This is the way we sweep the house
   So early Friday morning.

7. This is the way we bake our bread,
   We bake our bread, we bake our bread.
   This is the way we bake our bread
   So early Saturday morning.

8. This is the way we clap our hands,
   We clap our hands, we clap our hands.
   This is the way we clap our hands
   So early Sunday morning.

Oh! Susanna

Allegretto

I — came from Al - a - bam - a with my ban - jo on my
I — had a dream the oth - er night when ev - 'ry - thing was

knee; I'm — goin' to Lou - si - an - na, my — true love for to
still; I — dreamed I saw Su - san - na a - com-ing down the

see. It — rained all night the day I left; The
hill. A — red, red rose was in her cheek, a

Old MacDonald

With spirit

mf Old Mac - Don - ald had a farm,

E - I - E - I - O. _____ And on this farm he

had some { chicks, ducks, cows, } E - I - E - I - O. _____ With a

Lullaby

Gently
Play both hands an 8va higher

pp Lul-la - by and good night, with_ ros - es be - dight,_ with_ lil - ies be - decked is _ ba - by's wee bed. Lay thee

down now and rest, may thy slum - ber be blessed. Lay thee

down now and rest, may thy slum - ber be blessed.

Hush, Little Baby

Gently

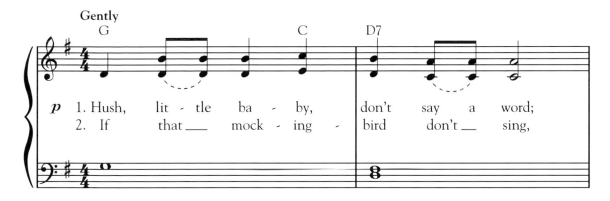

1. Hush, lit - tle ba - by, don't say a word;
2. If that ___ mock - ing - bird don't ___ sing,

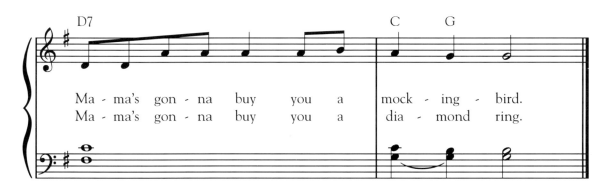

Ma - ma's gon - na buy you a mock - ing - bird.
Ma - ma's gon - na buy you a dia - mond ring.

3. If that diamond ring turns to brass,
   Mama's gonna buy you a looking glass.

4. If that looking glass gets broke,
   Mama's gonna buy you a billy goat.

5. If that billy goat don't pull,
   Mama's gonna buy you a cart and bull.

6. If that cart and bull turn over,
   Mama's gonna buy you a dog named Rover.

7. If that dog named Rover won't bark,
   Mama's gonna buy you a horse and cart.

8. If that horse and cart fall down,
   You'll still be the sweetest little baby in town.

Photograph of Grandmother and her Grandchild

Date _____

The Future

When you have a grandchild,
You'll have a good time, too.
Singing songs and sharing love,
Just like I did with you.

When I was a little girl I sang these songs with _____

_____

I enjoy when we sing together because _____

_____

The song you respond to the most is _____

_____

I get such a kick out of it when you _____

_____

You are a special grandchild to me because _____

_____

_____

I will always love you because _____

_____

_____

Index of First Lines

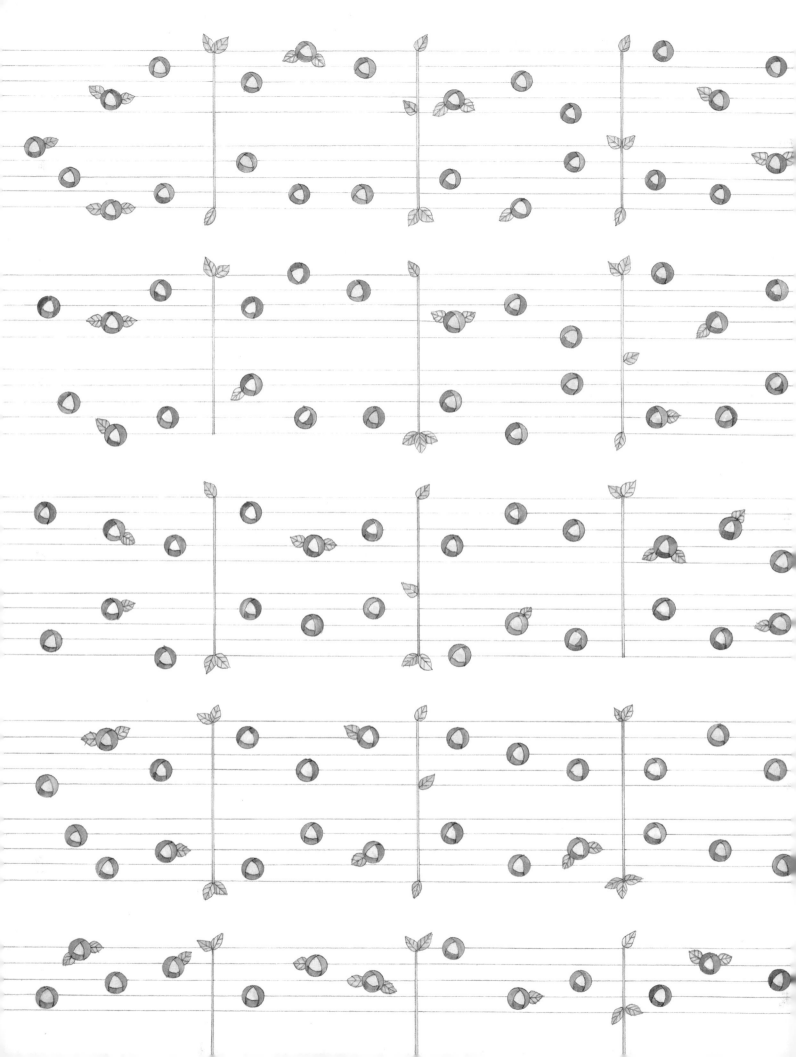